LANDSCAPE DRAWING IN PENCIL

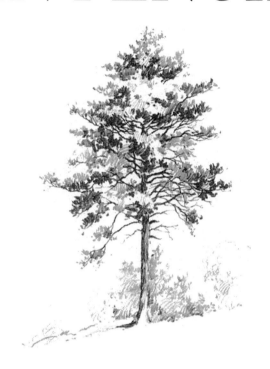

Frank M. Rines

DOVER PUBLICATIONS, INC.
Mineola, New York

Bibliographical Note

This Dover edition, first published in 2006, is an unabridged republication of the third (1937) edition of *Drawing in Lead Pencil*, which was originally published by Bridgman Publishers, Pelham, New York, in 1929.

International Standard Book Number: 0-486-45002-3

Manufactured in the United States of America
Dover Publications, Inc., 31 East 2nd Street, Mineola, N.Y. 11501

INTRODUCTION

Only recently has the pencil been considered by the laymen, as well as most artists, as anything more than a tool with which to sketch or map out ideas, layouts, etc. That pencils are ideally adapted to carry these ideas further—to carry them to completion in fact, will be obvious to anyone visiting our art galleries, or studying our recent books and periodicals, especially those of an architectural nature.

While closely allied with the other branches of Art, the pencil, like any other medium, necessitates certain methods or tricks in handling, peculiar to itself. A realization of the possibilities and limitations of the pencil is the first, and most important requisite to an understanding and appreciation of pencil work.

The purpose of this book is, not to make a finished "artist" out of everyone who chances to pick it up. Its aim is rather an appeal to those students, who have had some training and experience in drawing with other media—from the cast, we will say, with charcoal,—and especially some knowledge of free hand perspective (concerning which many excellent books are available)—to arouse an interest in the art of pencil technique, especially as it pertains to out of door subjects. If others,—those who are interested in art, in all its different aspects—are helped towards a better understanding of such work—then the reader and everyone who works with the pencil has been benefited.

The author does not attempt to establish any hard and fast rules as to technique, nor to imply that the examples shown here are the only way in which the pencil should be used,—for one of the beauties of pencil sketching is that there are as many different ways of working as there are persons to attempt it, and each student progressing in this work will gradually develop his or her personal technique, just as each one of us puts more or less of our individual characteristics into our handwriting. This of course, is as it should be, otherwise only a limited few artists would be needed to supply the entire demand for work of this nature.

A careful study of the following pages will, it is hoped, however, show how one artist has met and dealt with certain problems. The suggestions, principles, and few rules that follow have all been tried out with different groups of students and individuals. The results, naturally, have varied proportionately with the ability and previous drawing experience of each. In the majority of cases, however, the results have proved satisfactory, not only to the student himself, but also to the instructor.

"Copying" the examples given here is very inadvisable, but a careful study of each drawing is urged. After becoming familiar with the manner of holding the pencil, making the different strokes and the rendering of different materials, etc., as taken up in the first plates, the student is then advised to study carefully the following plates with the aid of the analysis accompanying each, explaining why this was done that way, and that was done this way, and to put himself, as much as possible, in the artist's place, applying his problems, as nearly as he can, to similar ones of his own.

Wherever practical, work directly from nature, but when, as is often the case, this cannot be done, good photographs may be used instead. In the author's experience with many different classes, working from photographs has been found to be very satisfactory, and it is highly recommended.

Constant and continual practice is the only sure way to succeed, in pencil drawing, as in anything else. To create the desire and determination to do this, and to help the student towards an ability to criticize his own work, which will develop step by step with his progress, is the author's wish. Needless to say, constant reference to the drawings reproduced here, as well as to those of other pencil renderers (of which the student should have many good examples) is one of the chief ingredients in the recipe for success.

LIST OF ILLUSTRATIONS

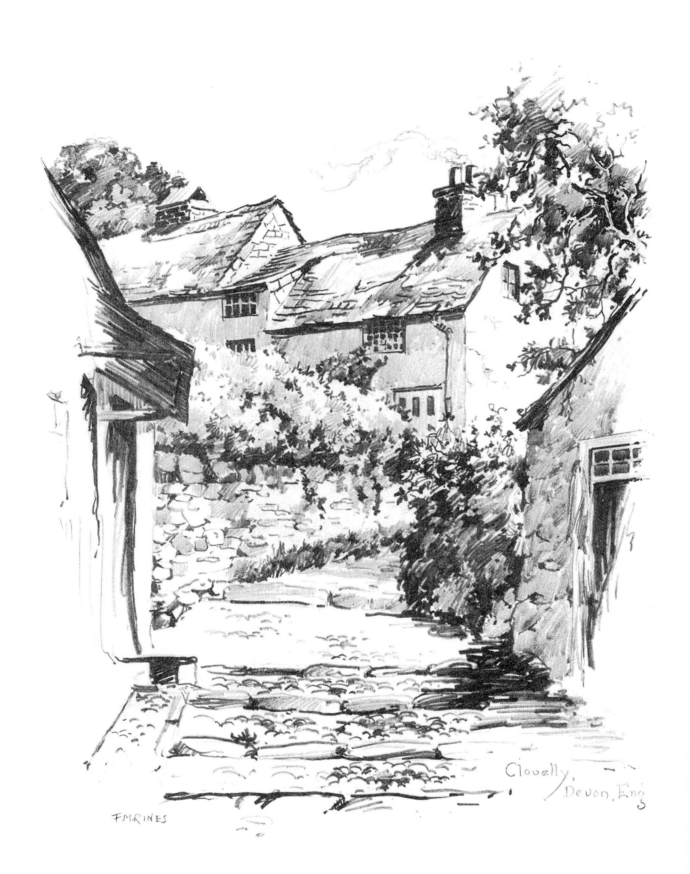

F.M.RINES

Clovelly,
Devon. Eng

DRAWING IN LEAD PENCIL

There are four important things to work for when drawing with the pencil. The first is correct drawing, the second, design, or composition. Of course, these are needed for successful results in any medium. The third; to be able to *leave out* all unimportant detail, and the fourth; to obtain contrast, sparkle, and "snap," are the goals for which the embryo pencil artist must strive. The eliminating of all that is not pertinent to the subject, is a stumbling block which retards the progress of every beginner, nevertheless it is an important element of all artwork; for, in spite of the variety of tones which the different grades of drawing pencils will produce, *simplicity,* so needful in bringing about contrast, prohibits the introduction of any but the essential or dominant features of the subject.

Merely reading this statement will not, perhaps, impress the student; but the fallacy of drawing everything he sees will gradually come to him as he progresses with his work. Therefore, we will dispense with further discussion of the matter at this time, but will bring it forward frequently, clothed in slightly different terms.

Technique is the outstanding point of pencil sketching which makes it so different in character from other media. The way the strokes are made is one of the most potent ways of making the drawing interesting. While the technique, when the sketch is completed, should not be so obvious as to blind the observer to the other qualities, yet the way the strokes are laid on is what constitutes the charm of a pencil sketch. The way in which the drawing is done, or built up, is one of the reasons for using the pencil in the beginning.

As stated in the introduction, it is presupposed that the reader has some knowledge and understanding of the principles of drawing and perspective, but that making finished sketches with the pencil is more or less new to him. Therefore, a certain familiarity with his materials and how to use them, is the logical first step. With this in mind, the following sketches and diagrams have been prepared. A conscientious study of these will bring home many facts, which mere words would fail to do.

It has been said that "a good workman never complains of his tools." Very true; but have you ever noticed that a good workman never *needs* to complain; that he always *has* good tools?

One of the most important things with which to start, is a drawing board, unless one intends to do all his work indoors, in which case a drawing or drafting table will do. In any event the wooden surface should not measure less than 14 x 20 inches. The reason for this will appear later. For paper, a smooth surface white Bristol Board of not less than three ply is necessary. This paper, which comes in a sheet 22 x 28 inches in size, may very conveniently be divided into four pieces of 11 x 14 inches each. There are several reasons for emphasizing this particular paper so strongly, one

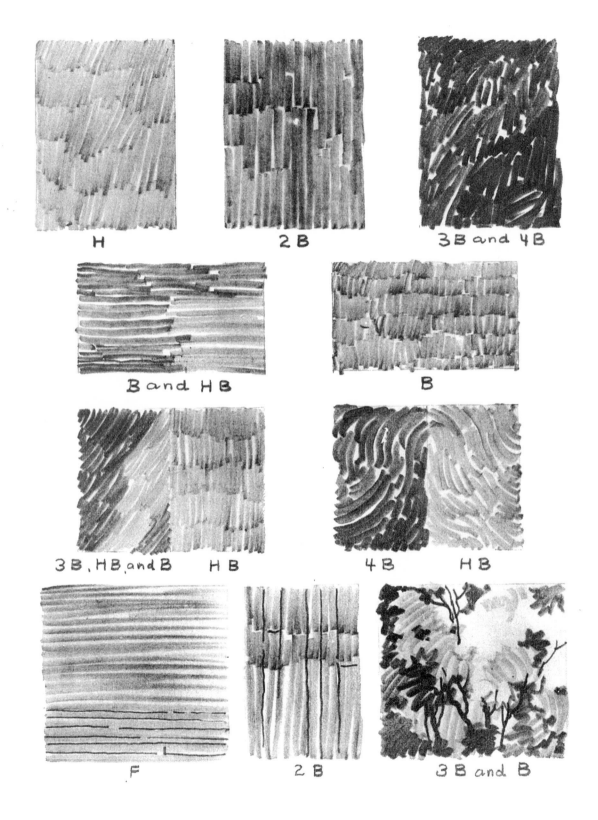

H   2 B   3 B and 4 B

B and H B   B

3 B, H B, and B H B   4 B H B

F   2 B   3 B and B

of which is its erasing qualities; no matter how much it is scrubbed, the surface is never impaired. Another equally important reason is its sympathetic response to every pencil stroke; while later on when the student has acquired considerable efficiency in rendering, he may experiment with other papers, it is predicted that he will never become fully weaned from the Bristol Board, when, by actual test, its value has been proven. All the drawings shown here were made on this paper, on the quarter sheets. The fact that they have been reduced to their present size should be borne in mind when examining the strokes.

The better makes of drawing pencils, of which there are several, come in a series of grades of hardness and softness. They range from 8 H, the hardest, to 6 B, the softest. For our purposes the 2 H, H, F, HB, B, BB, BBB, and BBBB are all that are necessary, but none of these grades should be omitted.

Besides pencils, paper, and board, three kinds of erasers are required; a kneaded, a medium hard, and a piece of Art gum. Something on which to wear down the points of the pencils, after they have been sharpened with either a sharp knife, or a razor blade; a piece of sandpaper, or better still, a "charcoal scratcher," as they are called, and a few thumbtacks complete the equipment and the student is ready to take the first plunge.

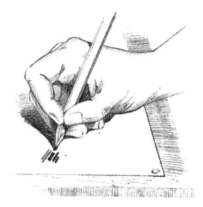

This first plunge, and many following it, should consist of practising the different strokes, in order to become thoroughly familiar with the "feel" of the pencil and to get acquainted with its possibilities. Prior to this, however, the pencils should all be cut as shown. Not more than 3/16 of an inch of the lead should project beyond the wood, but this lead should be left its full diameter, and not tapered. When all the pencils have been cut this way they should be held at an angle of about 45 degrees, and, on the sandpaper, worn to a wedge shape, as shown in the illustration. Before attempting to draw with them, run them over a piece of scrap paper once or twice, in order to remove all loose graphite. When this has been done, by holding the pencil as shown in sketch of hand, either the widest of lines (dependent upon the thickness of the lead) can be made, or also, the finest of lines, by turning the pencil so that only the edge touches the paper.

Of all the pencils mentioned, the 2H alone should be cut to a sharp point instead of the wedge shape, and used to lightly sketch in the outline and shadow shapes of the drawing. If these lines are drawn lightly enough, they

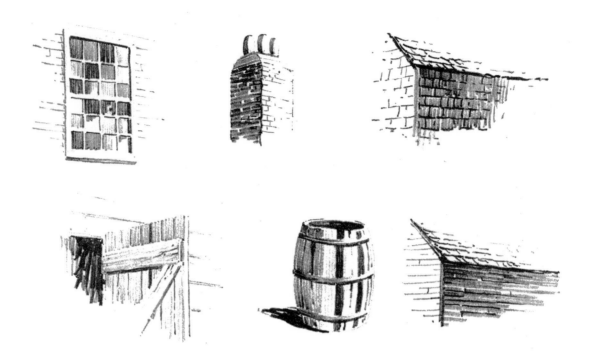

need not be erased; it is always better to lay in the construction lines lightly.

As a careful examination of the strokes will reveal, they have in all cases been made *direct,* that is, each stroke has been made in some definite direction, *and then left that way;* it has not been scumbled, or gone over again. In many cases, each stroke is distinctly separated from the others with a streak of white paper between; again, they have been placed so closely together that they give the appearance of a flat wash, or as if done with a brush. In any event the strokes must be made with decision; that is why plenty of time should be spent on just the practice of making them—short ones, long ones, straight ones, curved ones, separated and close together; before attempting to apply them in an actual composition. When a reasonable amount of efficiency has been achieved in making the strokes themselves, then the rendering of details is next in order. Not only those shown may be tried, but an infinite number of others, as they suggest themselves to the student.

When studying the various examples of strokes and details presented herewith it must be borne in mind that each specimen has been reduced to about one half the size of the original drawing; in other words, each stroke was originally made twice the size that it appears in the reproduction. This is true of all the small sketches, with the exception of the strokes shown on page 10; these are actual size.

The reduction of the plates that follow, as has been referred to previously, is to approximately two thirds the size of the original, which means that each stroke was originally half as wide again as it appears. A realization of this reduction is very important, otherwise the student is very liable to find himself deliberately trying to make strokes which are too thin, when instead he should be striving for more broadness of line.

Attention is called to the fact that, for the most part, the direction and character of the strokes is suggested by the material—in representing clapboards, for instance, the logical stroke is a long horizontal one, quite different from that used to represent bricks, which again, varies considerably from, let us say, grass strokes. Curved surfaces necessitate curved lines—flat surfaces either vertical or horizontal lines, according to their nature.

The use of the pencil requires a wrist movement, instead of an arm movement, like that of charcoal, or oil painting; hence, the dimensions of the drawing board, as previously mentioned, in order to insure a support for the wrist.

Most students (and many artists) make the mistake of using but *one* pencil, depending upon pressure to give variety to their tones. This is a serious error. The stroke should at all times be firm and crisp—enough to lay down the slight "tooth" which even the smoothest of paper possesses. It is best to keep the full set of pencils (already mentioned) at hand, selecting carefully which pencil is needed for each different line, or tone.

Let us now assume that some time has elapsed, and a certain familiarity with the pencil, and efficiency of stroke, has been acquired. We are now ready to attempt our first composition, either from nature, or a photograph. Much of its success will depend upon the selection of the subject. It should be fairly simple, of course, but aside from its simplicity, it should be one that is adaptable to pencil treatment. It is almost impossible to say what constitutes a good pencil subject; one just acquires such knowledge through constant observation. It is taken for granted that one who contemplates beginning the practice of outdoor sketching, has an inherent love for nature, especially its picturesque spots and bits. Since this is so, it will gradually become apparent that certain subjects lend themselves to pencil treatment more readily than others. One will soon find that wherever he goes, certain scenes will literally cry out "PENCIL" to him.

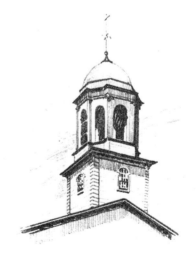

Having selected your problem, study it very carefully for a few minutes to determine just what is most striking, unusual, or interesting about it, and then by looking first at it, then at your blank paper, then back at the

[13]

scene again, try to visualize just how the finished sketch should appear and how the center of interest should be emphasized. Care should be taken not to have more than one center of interest. By placing your darkest darks, and your greatest contrast there, and by letting the drawing "vignette" or fade away on all sides, everything will be subordinated to this center. Do not attempt to "square up" the drawing; that is, do not draw a line around it, and then bring all the strokes flush with this line. Avoid any suggestion of straightness near any of the four edges, like a tree trunk, for example, and above all do not bring a branch of a tree or anything into the extreme corners. Doing this always makes the sketch appear too photographic.

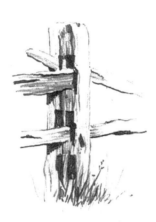

Draw in very carefully with the hard pencil, not only the main lines, but the outlines of all the shadow shapes, and masses, as well, so that when the rendering is started, the mind can concentrate wholly on the values and technique, and not have to concern itself with the drawing, besides. The more preliminary drawing that is done, the better the final results are bound to be. A good way to phrase it is to make an outline map of everything that is to be drawn.

Always be sure to have an extra sheet of paper under the one on which you are working, otherwise, when any pressure of the pencil is brought to bear upon the drawing, the grain of the board is bound to press through and affect the appearance of the strokes.

Some artists prefer to begin their rendering in the upper left hand corner, gradually working towards the lower right, so as not to have to move their hand over the strokes so much, while others commence with the center of interest, by indicating at the start the value and position of the darkest dark. No general rule as to procedure can be given; either way mentioned has certain advantages, and with practice, one way or the other will become more natural. In any case, a piece of scrap paper should at all times be kept under the hand in order to avoid smudging, and also to frequently test out the pencil strokes.

Under no circumstances should the pencil strokes be rubbed, or "stumped," as in charcoal, as this always destroys the fresh appearance, and makes a greasy looking tone.

Do not forget that we must have *contrast*, at any cost. Too much emphasis cannot be laid upon this factor for a pencil drawing without contrast, no matter how well it may be done in other respects, is an absolute failure. The ways by which such contrast may be obtained are legion, and as each drawing presents characteristic problems of its own, it would be useless to attempt to give any set rules for bringing about this condition. Some typical ways of producing contrast follow, however.

Always avoid a monotony of stroke. As has already been stated, the character of the stroke may largely be determined by the nature of the object being represented. A too short or choppy stroke is not as a rule desirable, yet at times, if used with proper discretion, it may serve as a relief from too many sweeping lines.

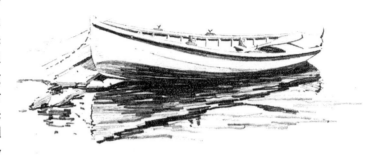

Examples of this may be seen in the rendering of shrubbery, brickwork, grass, etc. Remember VARIETY in strokes is just as essential to the spice of a pencil drawing as it is in life.

Bringing dark masses against light, and light masses against dark, at the center of interest, also affords an excellent means of contrast.

Extremely important, too, is the leaving of white paper. The parts of a drawing that are left white, or in other words, not rendered, are just as necessary as are the parts that are drawn. Only by leaving certain areas white, can sunlight or sparkle, be added to the scene.

The roof of a house, for instance, does not have to be made dark, simply because it appears that way, providing that for some special reason it should be left light any more than it should be light if it would obviously appear better dark. Suppose that in reality the roof is quite dark, but that behind it is a mass of dark foliage. How much more it will snap out if kept light, or even white. It is always easier to go back and tone down a space which seems too light, than it is to lighten up an area that is too dark; therefore, leave *plenty* of white paper until the final touches are being applied.

Undoubtedly, one of the most difficult things to draw, or paint, is trees and foliage. Many artists spoil an otherwise good piece of work by perpetrating what never did, nor could exist in nature, and calling it a tree. This whole treatise could well be devoted exclusively to the subject of rendering foliage and shrubbery, but lack of space forbids. That the matter receive more than passing mention though, is essential.

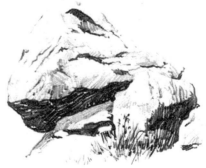

One reason why so many trees are poorly drawn, is because so few artists have realized the need for studying their formation and growth, both as groups, and as individuals. For anyone who is going to draw or paint out of doors, a thorough acquaintance with the ANATOMY of trees is just as essential as

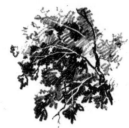

the knowledge of human anatomy when working from the figure. Each species of tree has certain marked characteristics, and each individual tree of each species has also marked characteristics, just as each individual of the human race has distinctive marks. The more one studies these marks of identification, and learns to be constantly on the watch for them, whether actually about to sketch or not, the more pleasure he will derive from nature. A very good plan is to make infinite drawings and studies of bare trees in the early spring, late fall and winter.

In the rendering of trees in particular, one should bear in mind the chance for variety offered by the *direction* of the pencil strokes. Different masses, light and shade, the way in which the twigs grow from the branches and the leaves from the twigs, may all be suggested by the way in which the pencil is handled.

Make a small hole about ½ inch in diameter, in the center of a piece of paper. Holding this near one eye, with the other closed, look at the middle of a mass of foliage (either in a photograph or in nature) (see sketch). Nothing but a green spot will appear; except for its color it might be anything, or nothing at all. Now move the paper so that part of the edge of the tree and sky show through the hole. Immediately the fact that you are looking at a tree becomes apparent. Now try the same test with any of the foliage in the sketches reproduced here.

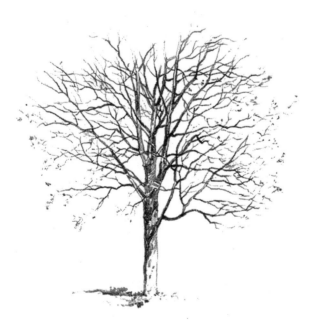

This proves that it is the *silhouette* that determines the character of a tree. Notice the difference between the silhouette or growth of different kinds of foliage; that of the elm and the maple, for instance (see plates). See how logical it is to bring out this difference by means of the pencil strokes.

Also remember that a tree is something *through* which the wind can blow, causing the leaves to tremble and rustle; therefore, keep the edges soft and lace like, and while not actually drawing each separate leaf, *indicate* the difference between foliage, shrubbery, etc., and building and masonry; in other

[16]

words, the difference between the growth of **nature** and objects made by man.

It is also advisable oftentimes, even though the tree from which you are working has exceptionally luxuriant foliage to let the sky show through, and to draw in a few branches and twigs. These should be made with considerable care, however, and conform as logically to the growth of the trunk as though the naked tree were being shown. Keep them of about the same value as the leaves; if they are too dark or heavy, they will stand out too prominently.

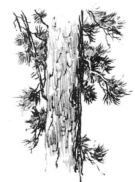

Great attention should be paid to the design, not only of the tree itself, but also of the separate masses. Frequently in nature, trees will be found to be ugly in shape. For example; one side will form too much of a straight line, or the foliage mass will appear unbalanced in relation to the trunk.

As an artist, whose purpose is to create a thing of beauty, why not change such ugly features?

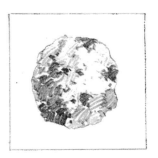 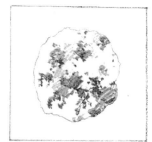

Another mistake that is frequently made, is to have the shape of a clump of foliage resemble some definite form, such as a dog's head, or other animal. Usually just a stroke or two will remedy this defect.

A few words as to foregrounds, another difficult part of the picture. Generally a few vigorous strokes of the softer pencils, applied in such a manner as to *suggest* the contour of the ground or water, will suffice. When rendering water, take great care that the strokes are either absolutely horizontal or vertical, otherwise the water will have the appearance of being uphill. Oftentimes the importance, as well as the proportion of some comparatively insignificant growth or object in the foreground has to be exaggerated in order to give distance to the scene. It is usually the difference between the flat washes and lack of detail in the background and the openness, boldness, and *suggested* detail in the foreground that gives what we call "aerial perspective" in a drawing. Be sure that the foreground, as the name implies, *comes forward.*

Before closing, a word or two regarding erasing may not be amiss.

When it becomes necessary to change some part of the sketch, a small piece of the kneaded eraser should be broken off, and well kneaded between the fingers, until it becomes quite moist. Then use this to lift off (not rub) as much of the line or tone as possible, before proceeding to use the other eraser, in the usual manner. The Art gum is handy chiefly to remove dirt and finger marks from the edges of the paper when the drawing is completed.

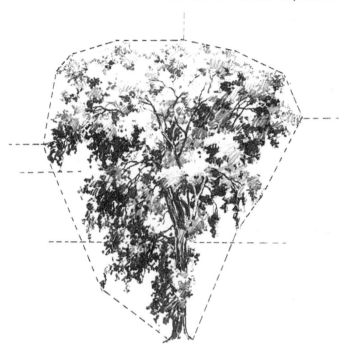

Once in a while, where it is necessary to have a fine white line against a dark tone, like a small branch of a tree or grass or reeds against a dark water tone, the sharp edge of some metallic substance (a coin, or key, for instance) may be used. Using great pressure, draw with this as if it were a pencil, making a sharp, indented line; then when the dark tone is put over this line it will stand out white, as the pencil will slide over it without leaving an impression. This is purely a "trick," however, and as such, should be resorted to very seldom. Used promiscuously, one's work is apt to appear too mechanical.

When a sketch is finished, if a piece of smooth wrapping paper is pasted over it, in the form of a flap, it is not necessary to "fix it." The use of "fixatif" is very liable to ruin the delicate gray tones of the pencil. If the drawing is first mounted, and the flap pasted to the mount, it will stand a reasonable amount of handling without becoming rubbed, or smootched.

A good way to do, if one intends to work much in the open, is to take the drawing board, already described, and nail on the back three narrow strips of wood about ½ inch square to the bottom, and the two sides. To these strips tack a piece of oilcloth, allowing enough extra at the top to form a flap. This makes a very convenient pocket in which to carry extra sheets of paper, as well as the finished sketch, and does away with the necessity for a portfolio. It has the added advantage, since it is waterproof, of protecting the paper when caught out in a sudden shower. The oilcloth can be very easily renewed, when it becomes worn.

In conclusion, the student must constantly be reminded that nothing but continual practice will bring to him the success which he desires. Do not be afraid to put down something on the paper; even if it doesn't look just right, the realization of the fact that it is wrong means that something has been learned.

Do not get discouraged; remember that others have had to travel the same road, along which there are no "short cuts" to the art of pencil sketching.

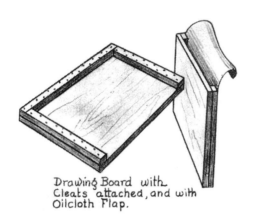

Drawing Board with
Cleats attached, and with
Oilcloth Flap.

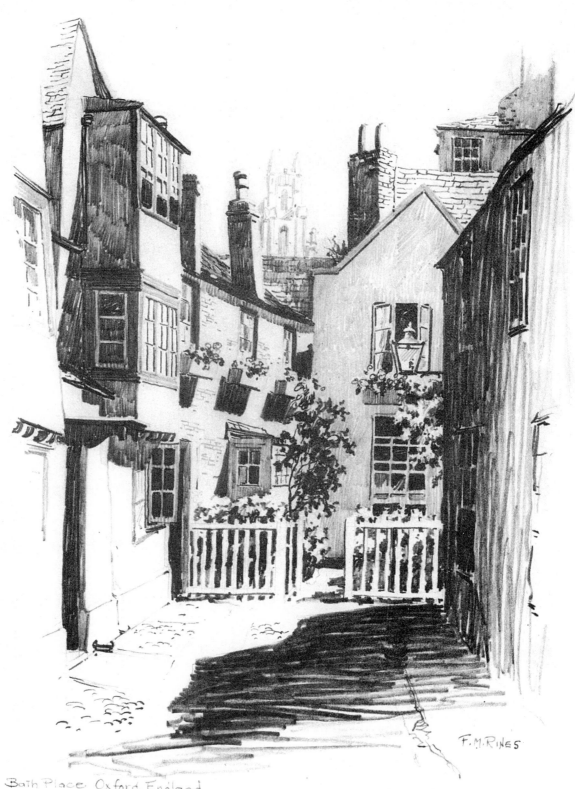

Bath Place, Oxford, England.

F. M. Rines

BATH PLACE, OXFORD

The absolutely smooth texture of the plastered, gabled end of the building in the center, admitted of but one treatment. The result is an excellent example of a smooth, flat gray pencil wash. Study it carefully, as well as the contrasting treatment of the building in front of it, on the right.

Observe how the whole drawing resolves itself practically into three tones, with the white paper of the building on the left forming one tone, that of the central building, already mentioned, forming the second, or intermediary tone, and that of the building on the right making the third, or darkest note. All the other values, with the exception of small areas of darker darks, used for accents, correspond to one of these three.

The tower in the background (one of the numerous college towers of Oxford) is drawn almost in outline, it being so distant, and unimportant to the rest of the composition.

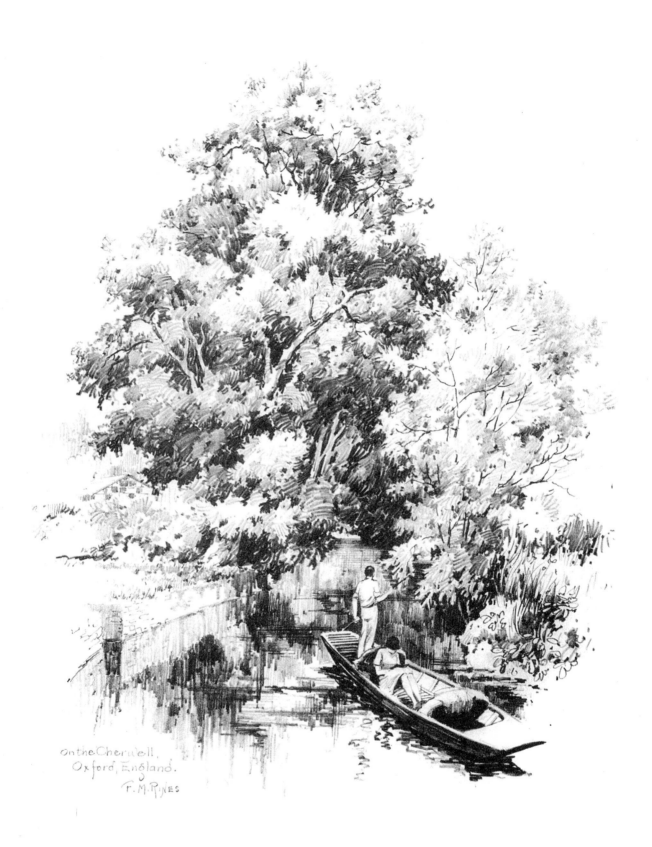

On the Cherwell,
Oxford, England.
F. M. Rines

PUNTING ON THE CHERWELL

The manner in which the tree on the right of this picture (a young willow) has been made to stand in front, or come forward of the trees on the opposite river bank was the most difficult problem in making this sketch. It is always one of the most·difficult matters to solve, and yet appears very frequently.

The more distant foliage was drawn first, and the dark tones brought up sharply against the solid outline of the willow, giving it the appearance of having been cut out from a piece of wood, with a jig saw. After this was done, the character of the silhouette was studied more carefully, working the darks into the white outline, taking care to get a variety of shape and spotting. Finally, washes of gray were applied to some of the foliage masses, in order to soften them.

Notice particularly how the strokes have been made on the larger tree, to bring out the different masses, or tufts of foliage, in direct contrast to the smaller tree, which being young growth, is naturally quite flat, in comparison. The branches showing through the foliage help to relieve what would otherwise become too much of a solid mass.

Study carefully the difference between the stroke used for the water and the trees.

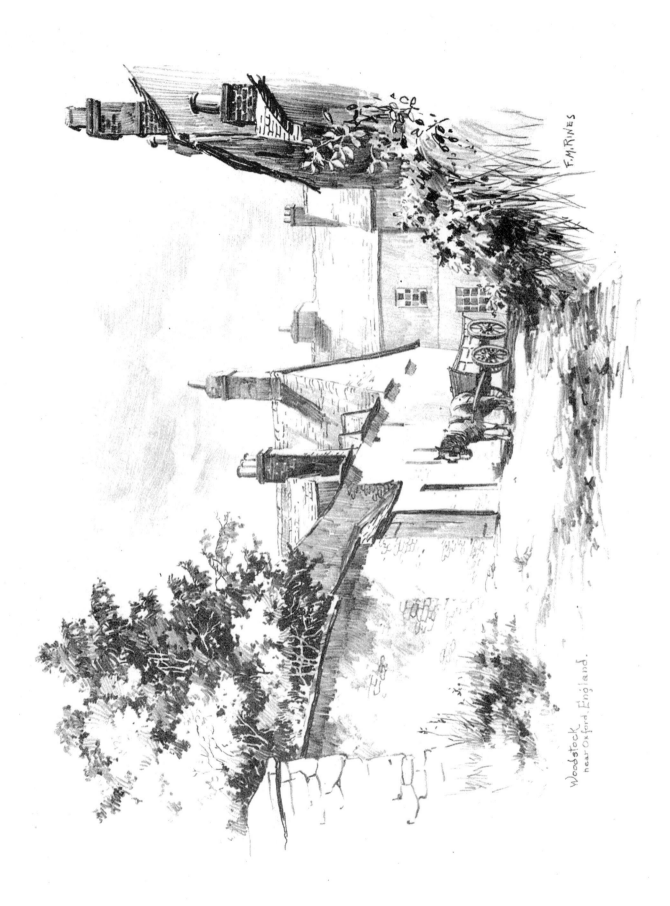

Woodstock
near Oxford, England.

F. M. Rines

LANE IN WOODSTOCK

The problem in making this sketch was to have the eye wander down the lane, without becoming sidetracked along the way. The greatest difficulty was to avoid making two pictures; that is, having either side interesting in itself with nothing to connect them. This problem occurs very frequently and will be found in several of the other sketches reproduced here.

The dark tones on the path in the foreground and the grass strokes on the left, combined with the shadow in the middle distance where the horse and cart stand, as well as the horse and cart themselves, all serve to carry out the connection between the two sides. Even the clouds in the sky help to tie the picture together, as well as to break up the otherwise white paper which would compete too strongly with the sunlit white walls of the buildings.

Note how the shadow side of the chimney directly over the horse's head is much darker than the higher one, beyond.

This is done in order to bring the darker one nearer, and as the farther ones are lighter still, they recede even more.

The foliage on the left offers a good example of leaving white masses in the trees.

Especial attention is called to the shrubbery in the right foreground. Some of the separate leaves are actually drawn. This brings them in front of the buildings, thereby adding depth, or distance.

The walls under the trees on the left were built of white-washed bricks, but it was necessary to suggest just a few of them. The bit of wall at the extreme left is left white and a few of the stones are drawn, their large size making it much nearer than the wall beyond it.

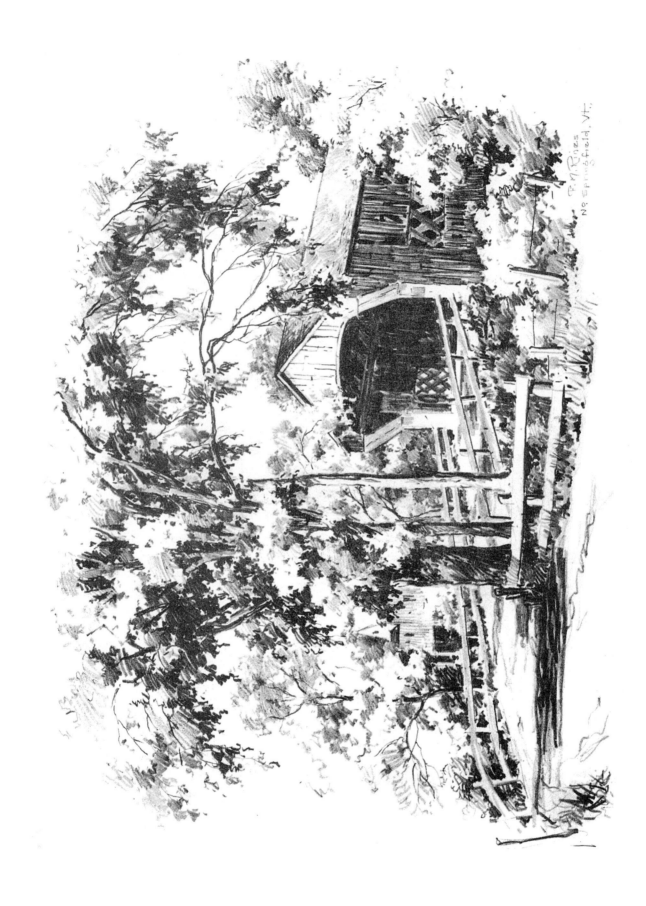

COVERED BRIDGE, VERMONT

As in the other covered bridge pictured here, the approach to it is one of its interesting features. Like so many other objects, a covered bridge, if taken by itself has little to recommend it, from the artistic viewpoint. Placed, however, amid a setting of natural scenery, half obscured by foliage, and the leading lines of the roadway and its accompanying white board fence, it becomes a subject at once picturesque and romantic.

The inevitable posters, announcing some travelling circus, plastered at the entrance, become an added attraction.

The manner in which the direction of the strokes conform to the growth of the leaves is especially evident in the large tree. On the left hand side the general direction of the strokes is *downward* from right to left, while on the other side they are *downward* in the opposite direction. For a person who is naturally right handed, the right hand side of a tree is always more difficult to draw than the other. The easiest way to make this stroke is with a sort of back-handed motion. A little practice and it becomes quite easy.

The branch of foliage in front of the bridge, serves the same purpose as in so many of the other sketches, notably the "OLD CHASE HOMESTEAD," where it is discussed.

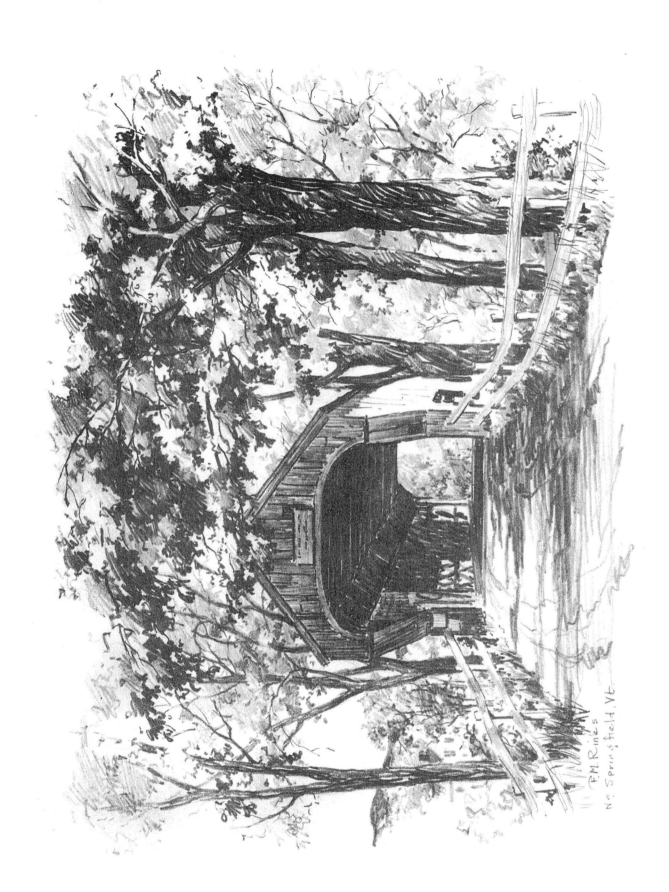

F.M.Rines
No. Springfield, Vt

OVER THE RIVER

A fine opportunity for observing foliage in a "close up" view is offered in this subject of a typical Vermont covered bridge. While none of the leaves are actually drawn, many of the coarse strokes are handled in such a way that they almost appear as individual leaves.

The sun, sifting down through the leaves is shown by the number of white clumps among the foliage, and also by the snappy treatment on the trunks.

The heavy shadow under the bridge, and the opening at the farther end, form a vista. The eye is led up to, and through the bridge to this vista by means of the wheel ruts in the foreground.

The trees in the background, on the right, are treated very softly, in such a manner as to make them recede, and yet soften the effect of the unusually black tree trunks to some extent.

Aside from its technical qualities, this drawing depicts what was once one of the most characteristic sights of rural New England, and what is still one of its most picturesque features. They are rapidly disappearing, however, due to the floods, and the demand, caused by increasing automobile traffic, for more practical structures.

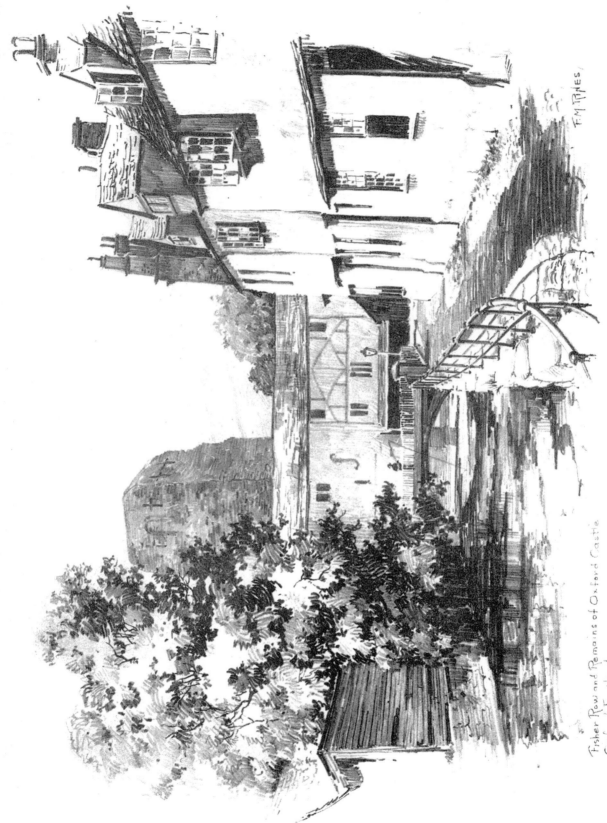

Fisher Row and Remains of Oxford Castle.
Oxford, England

F.M. Rines.

FISHER ROW AND OXFORD CASTLE

By far the most difficult part to render here was the tree. To avoid any straightness, or regularity of the silhouette required considerable planning, for the actual appearance was pretty much a straight line from top to bottom. Watch out for this in your own work; it is quite a common occurrence, and *must* be avoided.

The old tower, while quite gray in tone, has just enough of detail to show of what material it is constructed. The contrast between it and the buildings on the right, in brilliant sunshine, is quite evident.

Observe how the linear perspective of the iron railing and the tone of the sidewalk correspond; how the value of the walk lightens as it recedes, in harmony with the convergence of the rails.

The blackness of the doorway on the extreme right might appear inconsistent, but a dark spot there is very necessary as a balance to the amount of dark in the foliage and water opposite.

Often times this is the case, and one must be constantly watchful that his composition does not have an unbalanced, or one sided feeling.

The suggestion of movement, or current is evident in the water, in distinct contrast to the stillness expressed in some of the other water scenes.

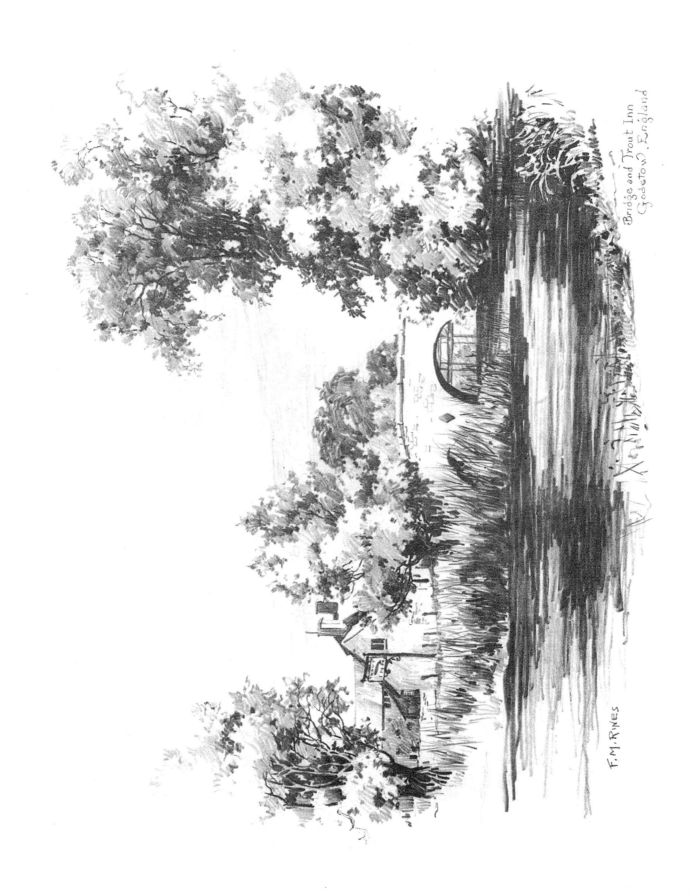

F.M. Rines

Bridge and Trout Inn
Godstow, England

BRIDGE AT GODSTOW

Very much the same condition existed in the trees on the right of this scene as that explained at some length in the Punting Scene on the Cherwell. In this case, however, the light mass of foliage, being of a much older and denser growth than that in the other sketch, the masses have been emphasized and for the sake of contrast the farther trees have been thrown more into shadow and therefore appear more simple.

A noteworthy feature here is a demonstration of how the strokes are governed by the material being represented, i. e. the long grass, or reeds in the center.

The bridge has been left practically white, but it is emphasized because it is so surrounded by dark tones.

Compare the water in this picture with that shown in some of the other sketches. The reason for its blackness is to add strength to the lower part of the composition. This weight is needed to balance the rather large proportion of sky space, and to offset the effect of what would otherwise appear as too much weight in the horizontal centre.

Its blackness also provides the opportunity for snapping out a bit the detail of grass in the lower right hand corner; just enough to bring the river bank nearer.

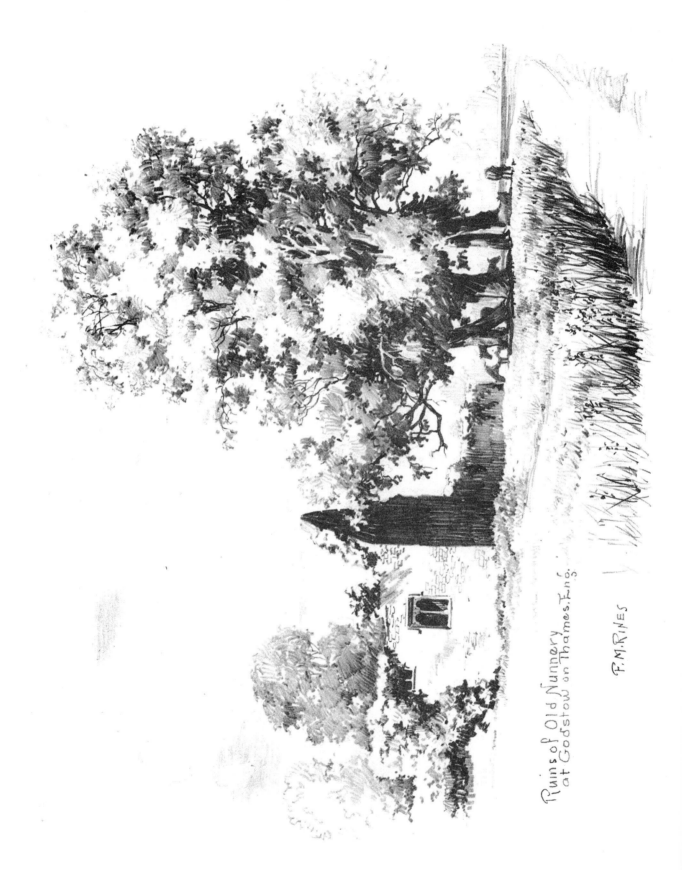

Ruins of Old Nunnery
at Godstow on Thames, Eng.

F. M. Rines

RUINS OF AN OLD NUNNERY

Among the several features in this drawing particularly worthy of study, the outstanding one is the group of trees. This was really the chief reason for making this subject; the ruins play a secondary part in the matter of interest. Note the design of the massing of sun-light and shadow in the foliage; also the lace-like quality of the edges as compared with the solidity of the central portion. While at first glance there appear to be but three trunks supporting this foliage mass, closer inspection will reveal five. In either case, three or five, they conform to the odd number grouping, spoken of elsewhere.

The trees in the background are almost poster like in treatment, to contrast with the finer, suggested detail effect of the main group, while the actual detail in the long grass in the foreground, brings this portion forward, a condition which must always exist if the drawing is to approach the appearance of the actual scene.

A few strokes to indicate clouds are needed in the upper left-hand section; otherwise too large an area of white paper would be shown, tending to counteract the white spaces so essential in other parts.

The blank space in the lower right corner is a tow-path along the river bank, although the water itself is not shown except for just a bit of gray tone in the distance.

The cows, grazing in the shadows of the trees, keep the scene from becoming too desolate.

Incidently, Fair Rosamond, the heroine of Sir Walter Scott's novel "Woodstock" is supposed to have been buried, in 1177, within the walls of this Nunnery.

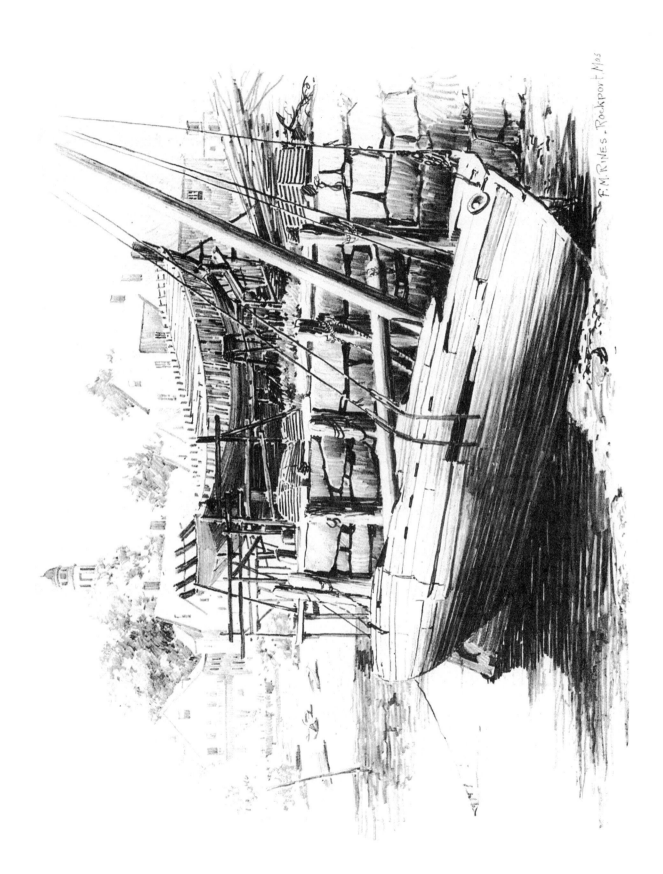

F. M. Rines - Rockport Mass

THE OLD AND THE NEW

The enormous amount of detail in this scene has been simplified as much as possible, but many different textures are still represented. The houses in the background are suggested with one tone and the white paper. The ship, under process of construction, is of a considerably darker tone than that used for the buildings, with just a bit of detail suggested here and there.

The old stone dock and its supporting piles, and the old boat, contain a good deal of detail.

Those three stages, or steps; the old boat and stonework, the new ship, and the houses, connected by the intermediate steps, such as the small boats on the beach, the water reflections, the lobster pots, lumber, etc., combine to give the appearance of distance, spoken of frequently in many of the other drawings.

The long, sweeping strokes on the hull of the boat in the foreground are in decided contrast to the short, rather choppy strokes of the water reflections, the stonework and the distant foliage.

The church tower, typical of so many New England towns, together with the solidity of the stone dock, the progress implied by the new ship being built, and the decaying hulk in the foreground, tend to give a romantic feeling in this picture; a result not always easily obtainable.

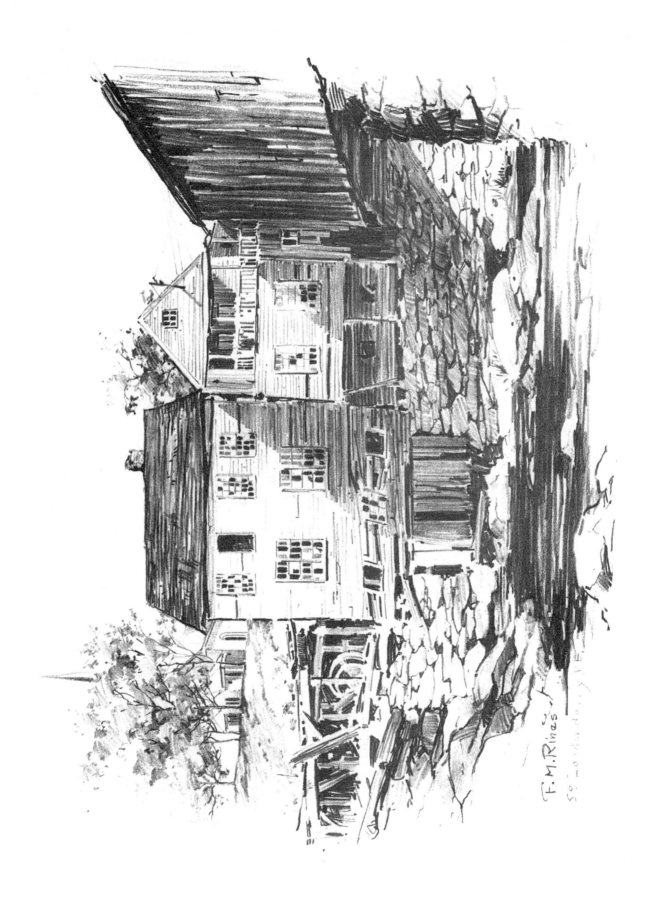

F. M. Rines

OLD MILL IN LONDONDERRY, VERMONT

The heavy tone on the extreme right, necessitated by the shadows on the covered bridge, is balanced by the snappy blacks and whites under the ruined platform on the left. Just enough black is contained in the broken dam, under this platform, to tie it up, or connect it, with the larger area of dark tones forming the shadows on and under the buildings.

The blackness of the 4B pencil in the water, brings it forward, as well as giving weight to the base of the picture.

The typical New England Village church in the background, is an interesting subject in itself, therefore, great care must be taken that it does not form a second center of interest.

The shadow on the wall was made by drawing the stonework first in white with the heavy accents and then running the shadow tone over it.

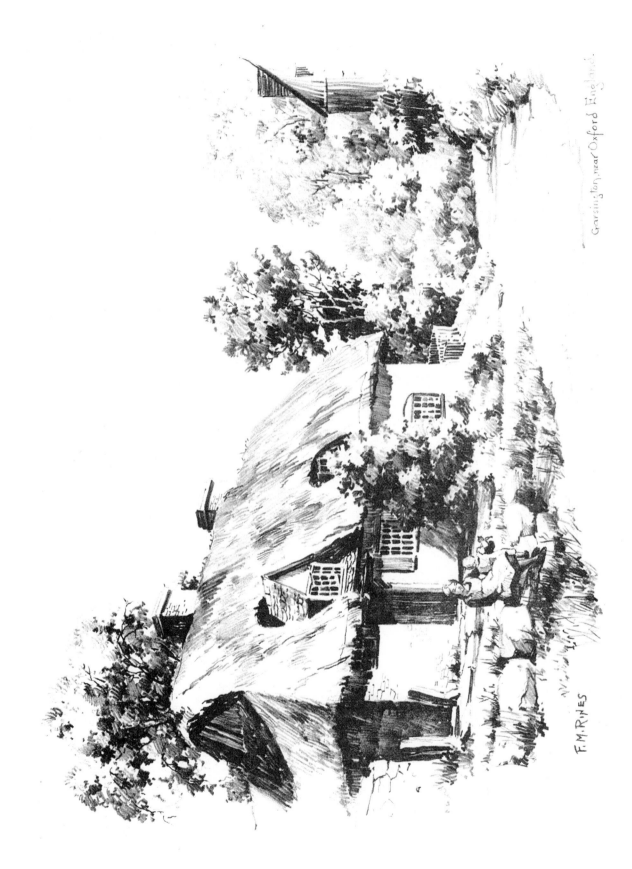

Garsington, near Oxford, England.

F. M. Rines

THATCHED COTTAGE, GARSINGTON

In this sketch the thatched cottage was the main object of interest, yet the country roadway was interesting, too. Cover up the right hand side of the picture and it will be seen that the cottage alone would hardly be of sufficient interest to warrant sketching.

In order not to detract too much from the house, however, the roadway was left almost entirely white paper and the more distant foliage was thrown into tone, in order to contrast with the detail of the cottage itself.

Notice the direction of the strokes on the roof. They conform to the texture of the thatch.

The nearer corner of the roof is snapped out white against the dark tones of the tree behind it, while the farther corner is a gray tone against the white paper of the sky. Doing this adds to the rather violent perspective line of the roof, helping to make the farther end of the building recede.

For the same reason, just a suggestion of brickwork, which showed here and there throughout the plastered sides, has been shown at the nearer corner.

Note the dormer windows with their slate shingles, and the way in which the thatch has been cut away around them. This gives a picturesque touch and makes the cottage different from many of the others seen thereabouts.

The figure in the foreground adds a human touch to the scene, keeping it from appearing deserted.

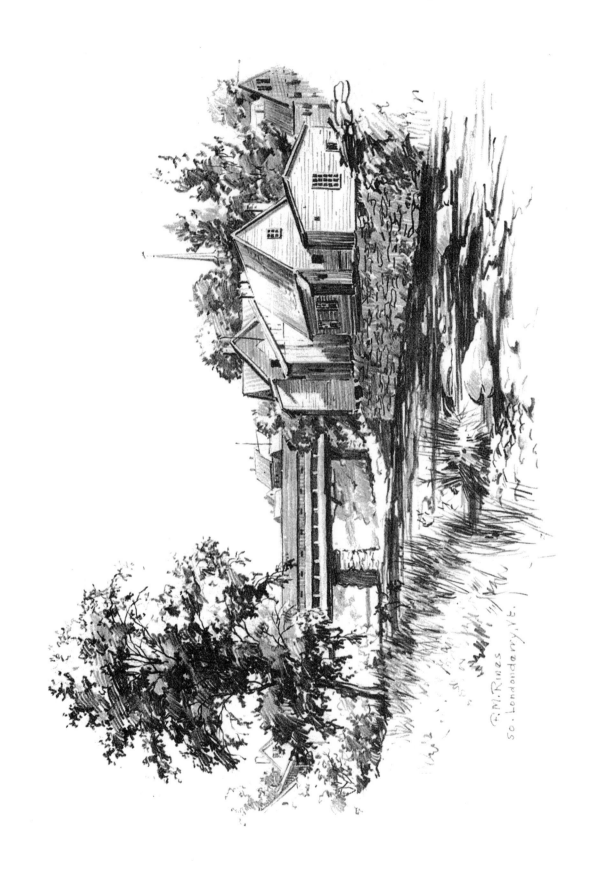

F. N. Rines
So. Londonderry, Vt.

WEST RIVER, VERMONT

Although at first appearances, a rather simple subject, an excellent opportunity to study strokes is offered in this sketch. The technique of the tree, for instance, because it stands out so clearly against the sky, becomes unusually evident.

The coarse grass in the foreground is indicated with long, vigorous strokes, made by starting the pencil at the bottom, following the actual growth upward, and letting the pencil gradually lift off the paper. This gives a tapering line, preventing the blunt ends that would result if the same pressure were used from start to finish of the line.

The technique on the buildings is quite simple, resolving more into a matter of pure light and shade, yet it will be observed that the strokes consistently follow the surfaces which they represent.

The full strength of the 3B pencil has been used for the water.

The river wall, although in shadow, has not been made too dark because it reflects a certain amount of light from the water.

The trees in the background have light and shade suggested, but are massed, and lighter in tone than the nearer tree.

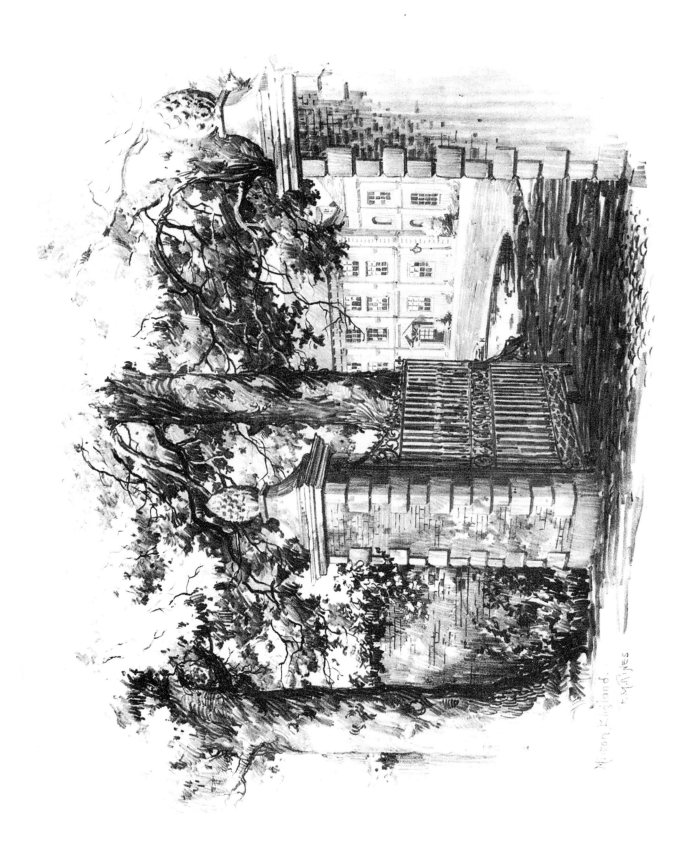

Milton Hartland.
F. M. HAINES

GRANGE GATE, MILTON, ENGLAND

The softer pencils were used for the dark green of the foliage and the brickwork, and shadows; for everything, in fact, except the house and bit of lawn in front of it. The H and 2H were used on these.

Doing this put the house in the background, or on another plane than the foreground, making a vista effect through the gate posts and trees.

Notice how a bit of the foliage and a dead twig have been drawn so as to cut the house. The contrast of these dark notes with the silvery tones behind them, creates "atmosphere" or space between them.

The shadow cast in the foreground by the trees adds greatly to the vista.

Particular attention is called to the pencil strokes on the tree trunks, denoting roundness and also, to the variety of strokes in the foliage. The branches and twigs emphasize how important it is to know "TREE ANATOMY" and to apply such knowledge.

This drawing affords an unusually good opportunity to study the difference in handling between the architectural and the natural textures, as well as one of the most difficult problems to be met with in pencil sketching: the "vignetting" of the edges.

Although the subject of this sketch happened to be in England, it is very much like many to be found throughout the eastern part of the United States.

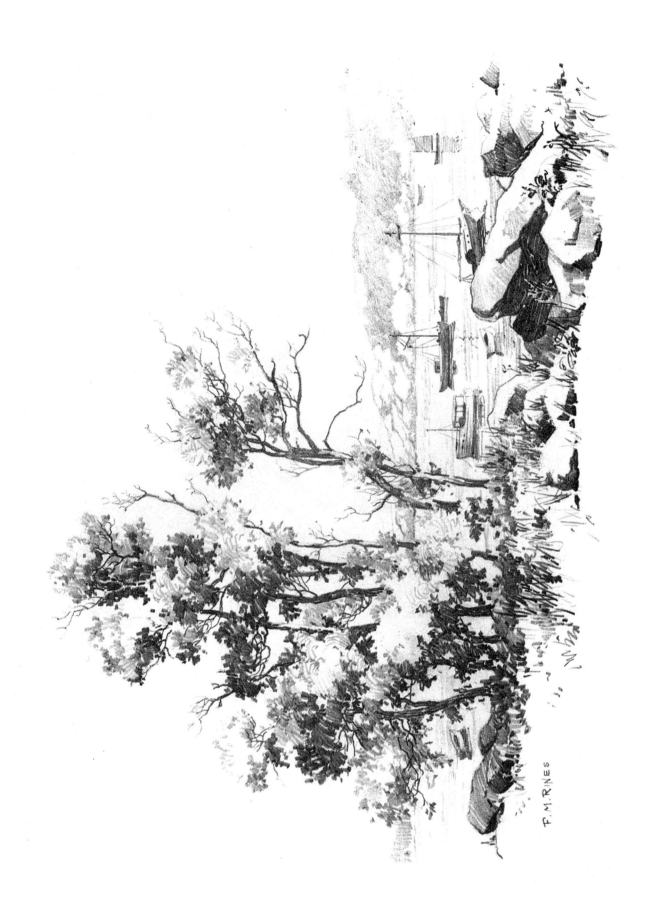

F. M. Rines

THE WILLOWS

A good example of the decorative quality of foliage is shown in this sketch. While, as previously stated, the design of the trees, as well as all the other elements of the composition should be given great attention, some subjects afford better opportunities than others for emphasizing this feature. The large amount of trunks and branches in proportion to the foliage, so characteristic of trees near the sea shore which are forced to bear the brunt of much stormy weather, helps greatly this decorative effect.

The opposite shore of the harbor is represented by flat gray washes, with patches of the white paper to indicate where the rugged and barren granite ledges crop out.

This same ruggedness, in much more detail, is suggested by the hard lines and sharp edges of the boulders in the foreground.

The last objects drawn in when making this sketch were the boats, as their values had to be gauged in relation to the tones of the background and foreground in order for them to assume their proper distance. Although the boats shown were only a few of the many appearing in the actual scene, note their variety, both as to positions and types.

Compare the large amount of white paper and "airiness" of this scene, with, for instance, that entitled "The Old and the New." This shows how one's subject should influence the treatment or handling of the sketch.

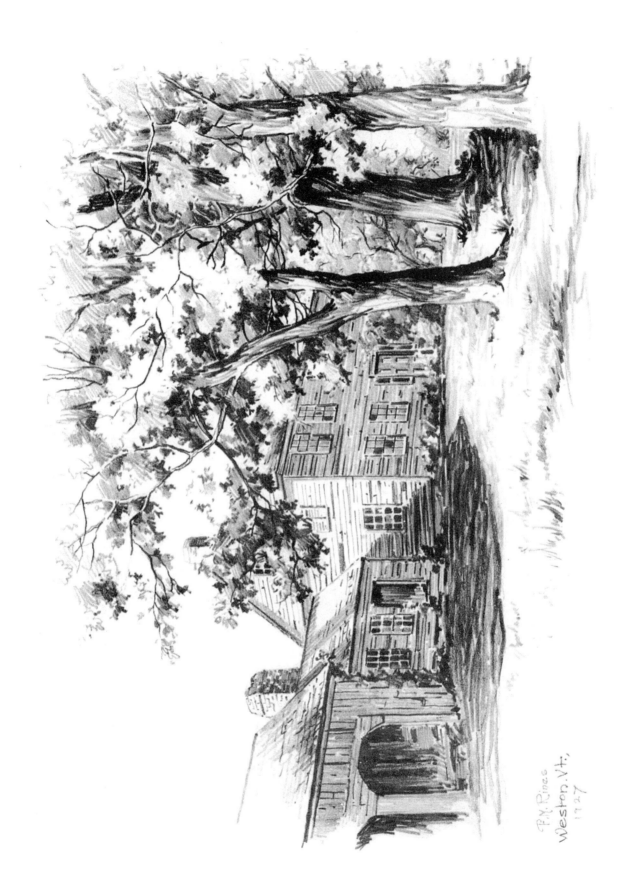

P. N. Rines
Weston. Vt.
1927

OLD CHASE HOMESTEAD

Notice how the *texture* of the weatherbeaten clapboards is brought out by the pencil strokes. Plenty of white paper is left between the strokes in order to give the shadow a luminous effect; in other words, to show the reflected light from the grass and foliage in front.

Compare the clapboard strokes with those used on the tree trunks, which are more on the curved order, to suggest the contour.

The dark branch of the tree which cuts the gable end of the house, helps to throw the building back. The large mass of white foliage brings it out in front of the other trees, keeping them from appearing too flat.

The white paper used to represent other masses of foliage, also carries out the effect of strong sunlight so apparent in the light and shadow on the house.

Particular attention was paid to the drawing of the tree trunks, the center one being at a different angle, in order to provide *variety* or *contrast*.

Notice that the cast shadows, that is, the shadows cast by the ell on the end of the house, and the shadows of the house on the ground, are darker in value than the direct shadows on the sides of the house. This is a good rule to bear in mind: that the cast shadows are always darker, the reason being that they do not catch any reflections.

So much tone, or weight has been used on the house and the foliage, that very few strokes are needed to just suggest the grass in the foreground: the same problem of contrast once more.

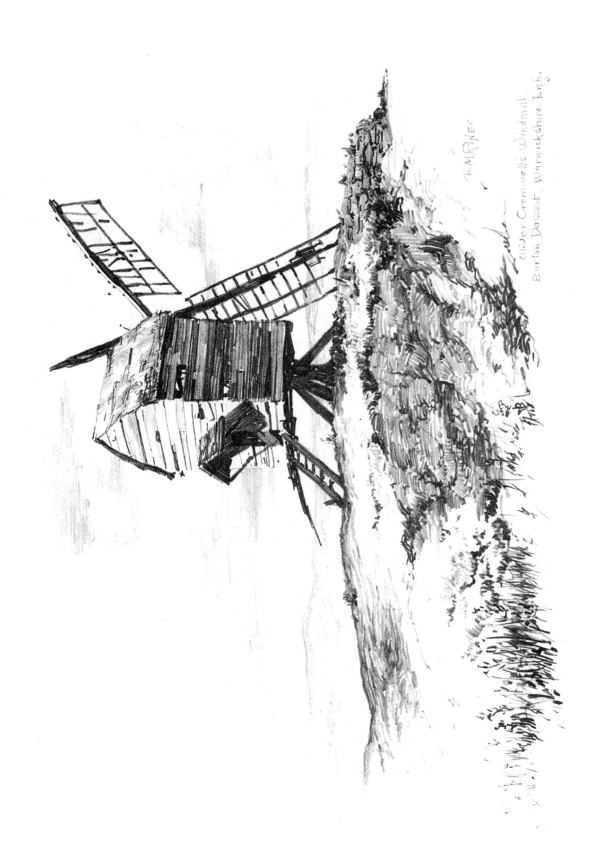

Oliver Cromwell's Windmill.
Burton Dassett, Warwickshire Eng.

OLIVER CROMWELL'S MILL

The most impressive aspect of this subject, as viewed in nature, aside from the interesting features of the mill itself, was its setting of loneliness and isolation. With this in mind, a position well below the floor level of the structure was chosen from which to sketch it. This allowed for plenty of sky space in the picture, and the clouds, the flat silver grays of the distant hills, and the broken and uneven foreground all tend to emphasize this feeling of desertion.

On the shadow side of the building, the *color,* as well as the light and shade has been indicated. A special study of the clouds and foreground is urged. Since the subject of the picture, the mill, is so comparatively simple and lacking in detail, more work is needed in the foreground, a condition exactly the reverse of that met with in many of the other sketches shown here. For instance, compare the center of interest of this subject with that of the row of half timbered houses at Chiddingstone, where almost no foreground has been indicated.

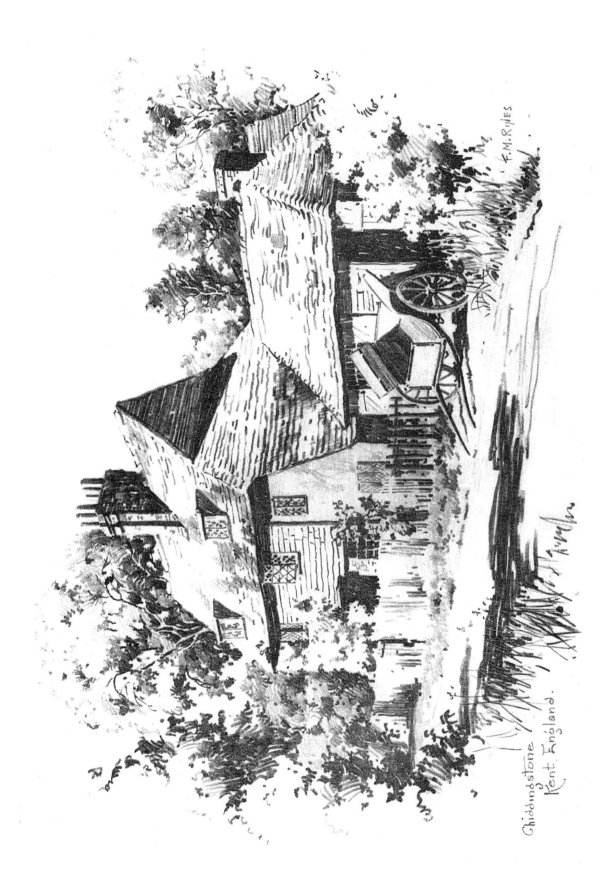

Chiddingstone
Kent. England.

F. M. Ryles

A CHIDDINGSTONE COTTAGE

Compare this drawing with the Thatched Roofed Cottage at Garsington. Aside from the different architectural features, the two problems might be construed to be the same. And so, to a certain extent they are, inasmuch as both contain about the same subject matter; a house, some foliage, and a roadway. But this picture might almost be entitled "A PORTRAIT OF A HOUSE," while the other is obviously a *scene*. The difference is that this house, possessing so much more architectural detail than the other has been centered more, making the background and foreground more subordinate. That does not mean, however, that they should be neglected. Just as much care has been taken with what might be called the "accessories" in this sketch as in the more prominent trees, grass, etc., of any other, only they have been simplified a little more.

Notice how the roofs (all tile) have been handled in order to avoid a monotonous effect. Note also how that part of the wall of the cottage which is of plaster has been drawn so as to contrast with that which is of wood.

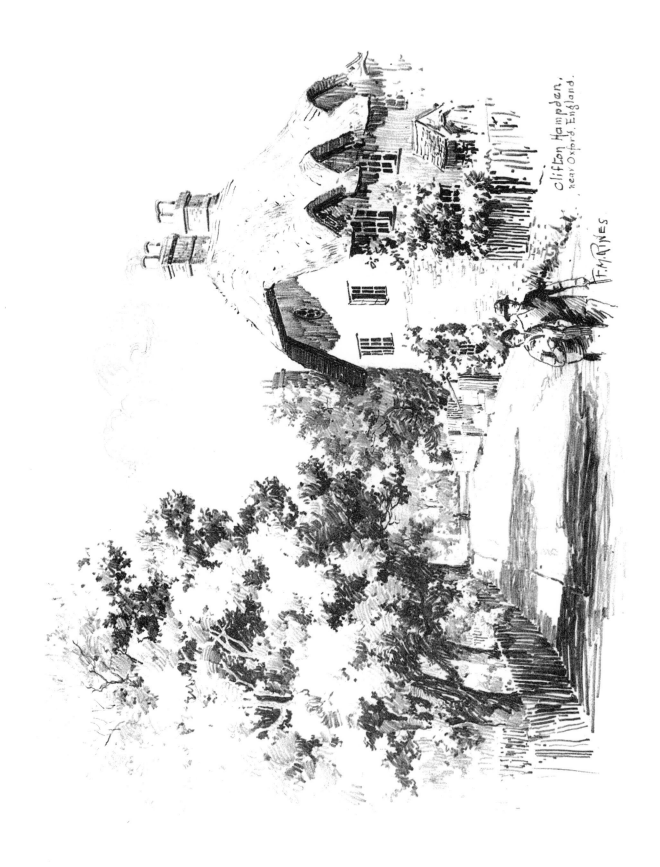

Clifton Hampden,
near Oxford. England.

F. M. RINES

COTTAGE AT CLIFTON HAMPDEN

A peculiar feature of the thatched cottage in this scene needs a word of explanation. The end and side pictured were not at right angles to each other, hence the peculiar perspective. Aside from this peculiarity, there are several other interesting details; the way, for instance, the upper portion is of plaster and the lower half is of brick construction, also the different angles at which the two chimneys face.

The way the tufts of foliage catch the sunlight, causing great contrast between them and the holes, in deep shadow, makes a group of trees as interesting as the house itself.

When such a case occurs, as it does quite frequently, great caution must be taken to avoid a "two-in-one" effect. The shadows across the roadway, just touching the two figures, which in turn cut the base of the cottage, the light gray massing of the foliage in the background, and even the *direction* of the wispy smoke, all tend to pull the composition together and make *one* picture of it.

Note the difference in value between the shadows of the trees in the road. Although to the eye their difference, in reality, was so slight as to be indistinguishable, they must be drawn as they appear here; otherwise the ground would appear vertical instead of flat, or level.

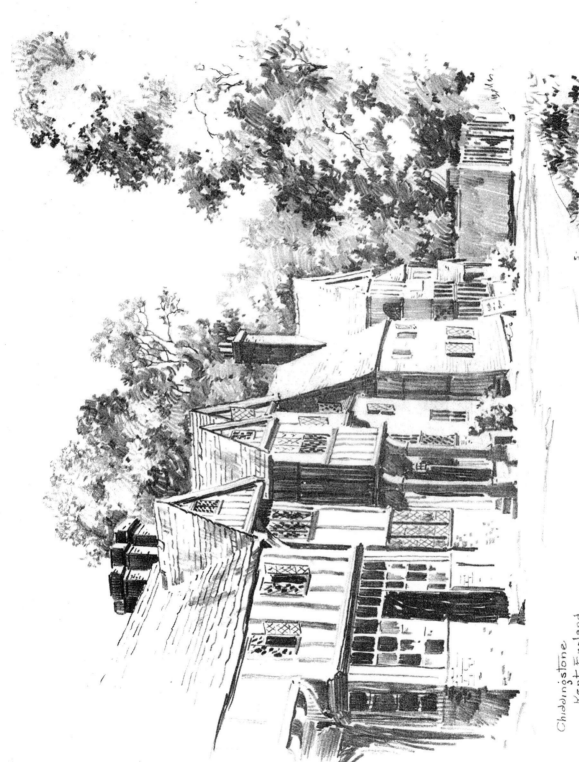

Chiddingstone,
Kent, England

F.M.RNES

HALF TIMBERED HOUSES IN KENT

This long row of buildings, with the massed foliage behind them, is interesting on account of its variety of architectural detail. Even the three gables near the center of the row are different in proportion and height.

Notice the snappy blacks in the doorway and window panes of the nearer house and the comparatively lighter tones of those in the distance. As in the other drawings reproduced here, this is done in order to obtain the perspective or receding appearance.

See how the lights of glass in the shop windows in the foreground have been broken up by making them different tones. This does not necessarily indicate broken glass, but shows, as so often occurs, the reflections, either of the clouds or foliage, and prevents the mechanical look which would otherwise exist. The same idea has been carried out, to a lesser degree, in the small latticed windows.

A suggestion of the slate shingles on the light roofs is all that is needed, for the foliage and the shadows of the nest of chimneys bring out the broken up roof lines sufficiently.

The vignetting of the tree on the one hand and the house on the other prevents a harsh line on either side.

Practically no foreground is needed here, as in several of the other sketches, for reasons already explained.

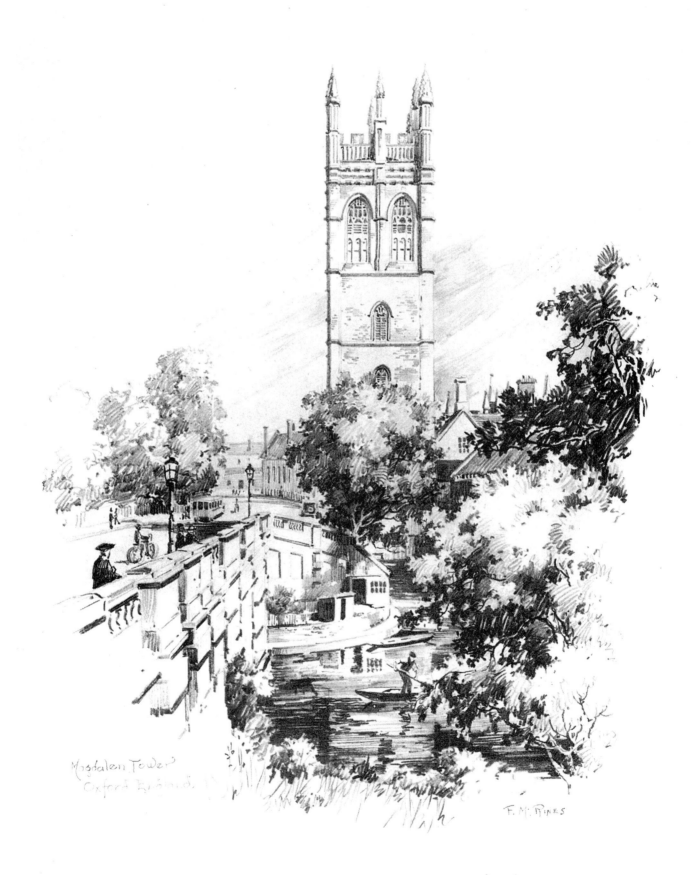

Magdalen Tower
Oxford England

F. M. Rines

MAGDALEN TOWER, OXFORD

Probably more familiar, due to the fact of its being pictured so often, than any other subject shown here.

Observe that the tower has been placed just the least bit removed from the center of the composition. To avoid a harshness of line, and to give it its real appearance of softness against the sky, the light clouds have been used to form part of the right hand edge, and where no clouds have been shown the white paper of the tower has been allowed to merge into the white paper of the sky. The horizontal lines stopping abruptly, as they do in conjunction with the clouds, complete the appearance of an edge, which is all that is necessary.

The different tones of the foliage, as it appears in its several different planes, might be described as a series of steps. The tree immediately in front of the base of the tower appears nearer than the trees across the street, on the left, by reason of its darker tones. While both the trees on the right are on the nearer river bank, the lower one, by reason of the white paper left in it, comes in front of the darker, higher one, which in turn, on account of its darkness and coarser handling comes much nearer than the one on the opposite bank.

For the same reasons, the reflections in the water, and the contrasting white of the shrubbery on the bank, have been drawn. In contrast to all of this, are the light gray tones of the buildings up the street, beyond the tower.

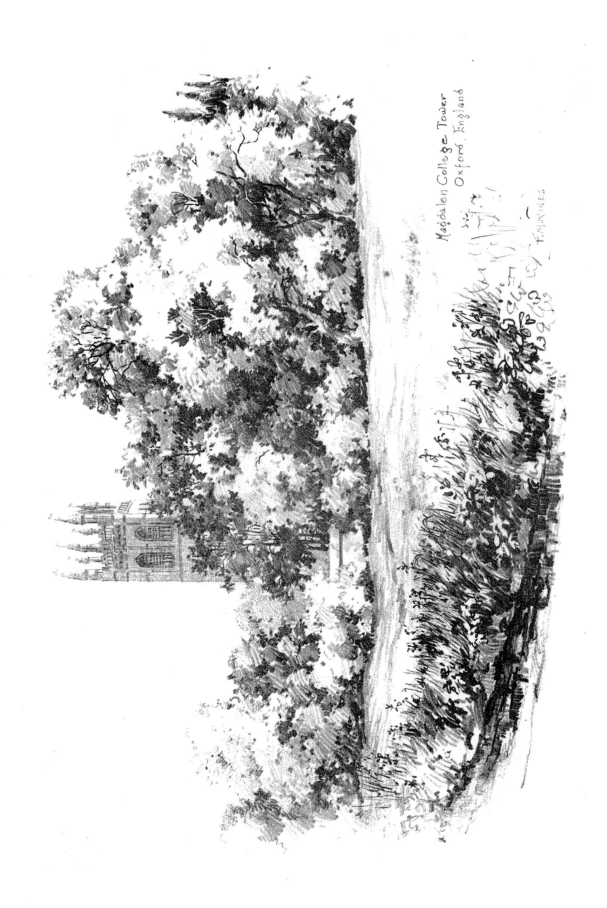

Magdalen College Tower
Oxford, England

by FAIRINGS

MAGDALEN TOWER FROM THE MEADOW

A conscientious study of the masses of white paper in the foliage of this scene is urged. By leaving a generous amount of these white masses, both sunlight, and a sense of three dimensions; i. e., *depth*, as well as height and length, has been obtained. These effects are impossible to produce otherwise. As in every case, the white areas stood out very sharp and definite at first; the gray tones, or modelling were added later.

A few leaves in detail, among the growth along the bank of the stream in the foreground, make them appear very close, in contrast to the entire lack of any such detail in the trees.

A few broad strokes of the pencil have sufficed to indicate the uneven contour of the meadow land.

The tower, while certainly of interest, is so on account of its silhouette, rather than detail, hence the flat wash treatment, with a slightly deeper tone for the windows.

A subject of this nature, with its preponderance of foliage is much more difficult to render than those in which architecture, in one of its various forms, predominates. For that very reason, such subjects should not be avoided, but attempted over and over again, until gradually, they can be made with as much facility as the others.

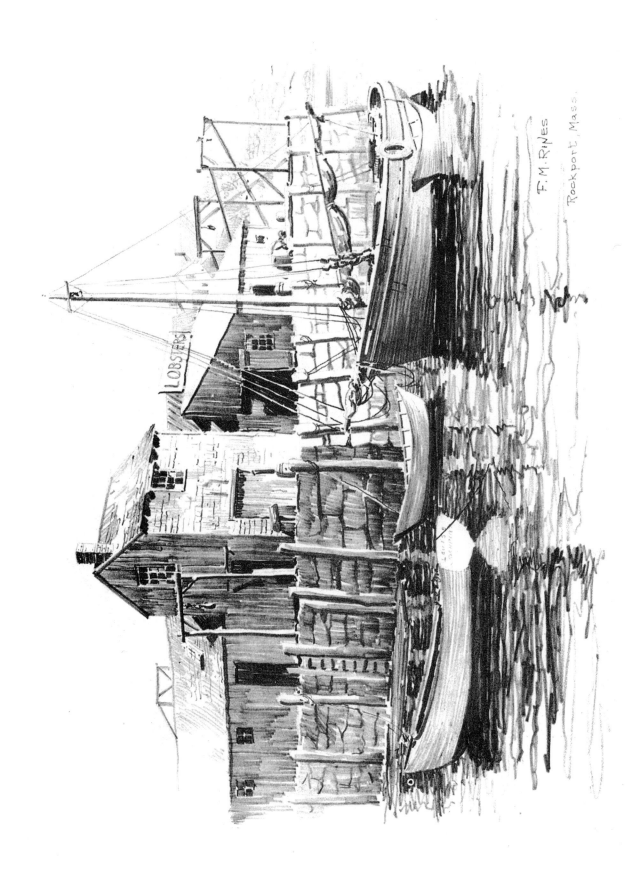

LOBSTERS

F. M. RINES

Rockport, Mass.

THE FISH WHARVES, ROCKPORT

To those who are fortunate enough to live along our New England seacoast, or to have access to it during the summer months, no other subjects are better adapted to pencil treatment than those similar to the one shown here, i. e., old fish-houses, docks, and boats, together with the accessories always to be found in such an environment. The textures of the shanties, usually either unpainted weather-beaten boards or shingles, lend themselves unusually well to the quality of tones which the pencil produces, and so to quite an extent, do the rocks, piers, boats, water, lobster pots, etc.

Notice the difference in value between the reflections and the objects themselves. Observation will confirm the fact that reflections, no matter how clear, are darker in tone than the objects casting them.

Like the boats in "The Willows" scene, the placing of those in this sketch have been very carefully planned. This planning necessitated the elimination of some actually there, and the introduction of one or more of those nearby, in order to provide variety.